Study Guide

CLASSIC CHRISTIANITY

BOB GEORGE

D0089840

HARVEST HOUSE PUBLISHERS
Eugene, Oregon 97402

CLASSIC CHRISTIANITY STUDY GUIDE

Copyright © 1990 Harvest House Publishers
Eugene, Oregon 97402

ISBN 0-89081-845-2

Contents

• • • • • • • • • • • • • •

Introduction

● ● ● ● ● ● ● ● ● ● ● ● ● ● ●

It is our human tendency to turn what should be a vibrant personal relationship with the living Christ into a religion. We continue to stray away from the basics, to substitute good things for the best things, to become encrusted with the barnacles of tradition, to wander away from our first love. It happened to me.

I forgot what I told hundreds of people in evangelistic appeals: "Christianity is not a religion. It is a relationship with God through His Son, Jesus Christ." I strayed from Christ to the "how tos" of Christianity. I taught seminars on how to share your faith. I developed philosophies and principles for discipleship, and methods and strategies to effectively lead small-group Bible studies. All this was wrapped up in a big package with the words "innovative," "creative," and "culturally relevant" stamped on the outside. It sounded so good.

But with all my "how tos," methods, and strategies, I lost sight of the reality of trusting Christ to live His life in and through me. I became burned out and lost the joy of my salvation. Starting out with great enthusiasm, I became disappointed and unfulfilled, ending up merely "going through the motions." I write all this to say that this study guide is not a "how to" manual for the Christian life.

In *Classic Christianity* I wrote about my journey to rediscover "the real thing." It was the journey I took through the Scriptures and through real-life experiences. I wanted reality in my life, and more than anything else I wanted to know more fully the person of Jesus Christ.

The purpose of this study guide is to help you understand "how wide and long and high and deep is the love of Christ, and to know this love that surpasses knowledge—that you may be filled to the measure of all the fullness of God" (Ephesians 3:18,19). This journey begins in the Scriptures. The Bible tells us that "faith comes from hearing, and hearing by the word of Christ" (Romans 10:17 NASB). It is the Word of God that is "living and active." It is the Word of God that gives substance to our lives, that transforms our hearts. *It is the Word of God that points us to Jesus Christ.* And it is in Him and Him alone that we find life and discover "truth that will set us free." Study each of the passages carefully, answer each of the questions, and humbly allow God to teach you His unconditional love and the reality of Christ living in you.

This study guide also includes many of the stories and illustrations presented in the original book. These stories are there to provide hope, showing that Christianity is not pie-in-the-sky theory, but is a life that is real and can be experienced here and now. You will identify with many of the trials, tribulations, and struggles that I and others have experienced. But the real lesson to learn through each story is that we have a God who loves us perfectly. We can depend upon and trust Him to complete the work He began (Philippians 1:6).

The apostle Paul wrote 1900 years ago: "But I am afraid that just as Eve was deceived by the serpent's cunning, your minds may somehow be led astray from your sincere and pure devotion to Christ" (2 Corinthians 11:3). Classic Christianity has been neglected, buried, and rediscovered countless times through the centuries. It has burst forth wherever there have been individuals with a sincere desire to know the reality of Christ. The deepest prayer of my heart is that God will use this study as part of His movement to call His people back to Classic Christianity in our time.

> To them God has chosen to make known among the Gentiles the glorious riches of this mystery, which is Christ in you, the hope of glory. We proclaim him, admonishing and teaching everyone with all wisdom, so that we may present everyone perfect in Christ. To this end I labor, struggling with all his energy, which so powerfully works in me (Colossians 1:27-29).

1

• • • • • • • • • • • • • • • • • •

Busy
and Barren

• • • • • • • • • • • • • • • • • •

Lord, Take Me Back

It was another Monday morning, and I was inching my way down the expressway to one of the busiest schedules imaginable. My eyes clouded up with tears as I cried out, "Lord, take me back to the days when I first knew You." I had lost the joy of my salvation.

Perhaps you are crying out in your own way, "Lord, take me back to the days when I first knew You." Through the following questions and illustrations you will see the many reasons why the joy of our salvation slips away.

Doing the Right Things

Mac was a hard-driving businessman, 70 years of age. He realized that he had never personally trusted Christ. The pastor greeted Mac as he walked down the aisle to publicly profess his faith in Christ. The pastor exclaimed, "This is one of the most brilliant businessmen in our city. He's wealthy, talented, and we need to put him to work."

Mac, with tears in his eyes, looked up at the pastor and said, "Pastor, I don't need a job. I need the Lord."

In John 6:28, what was the question the disciples asked Jesus?

_____

What was His response in verse 29?

_____

_____

Read the story of Martha and Mary in Luke 10:38-42.

What is Martha's complaint to Jesus?

_____

_____

How does He respond?

_____

_____

According to this story, what would you say is the priority of the Christian life?

_____

_____

In the illustration about Mac, what was wrong with the pastor's comments?

_____

_____

What does Mac's response say about our true need as Christians?

_____

_____

God's Wooden Spoon

Mary grew up in a strict denomination where she learned to be afraid of God. Her whole life she carried the burden of sin on her shoulders. Until learning about God's grace and total forgiveness, she constantly looked over her shoulder to see if God was running after her with His great wooden spoon.

According to Romans 5:9, what are Christians—those justified by His blood—saved from?

_____

What does John say fear is related to in 1 John 4:18?

_____

What did Mary fear before she came to know God's grace and total forgiveness?

_____

_____

Will a person ever experience the joy of the Lord if he or she is fearful of being punished by God?

_____

How do people act when they fear being hit with God's wooden spoon?

_____

According to Galatians 3:10, what is the result of these efforts?

_____

_____

How are we justified according to Romans 5:1?

_____

How does Romans 5:1 apply to our lives when we struggle with guilt and fear?

_____

_____

Answers Learned on the Expressway

The Christian life can be real. It doesn't have to be an act—pretending you are doing great, when deep down you know something is wrong.

Through the tears I shed while driving on the expressway, God led me to the answers I was looking for. Through your tears and hurts, God can lead you to truth that will set you free.

Truth Sets You Free

Read John 8:31-36.

Why does John tell us to abide in God's Word?

_____

What is the result of knowing truth?

_____

_____

If truth sets you free, what puts you in bondage?

_____

If you are in bondage today, what is the reason according to this passage?

_____

Christianity: A Relationship, Not a Religion

When I first received Christ, I could hardly wait to read the Bible. My wife said I had a black-leather face. But soon my sincere love of Christ was exchanged for a desire for theological knowledge. Even in something good, I had strayed from my relationship with Christ.

What does 1 Corinthians 8:1 say that knowledge does?

_____

Many of us read the Bible for knowledge. What does 1 Corinthians 8:2 say about the person who is enamored with his own knowledge?

_____

In John 8:31,32 what does John say will set you free?

_____

In John 8:36, who sets you free?

_____

What two qualities does John 1:14 say Jesus possesses?

_____

In John 5:39,40 to whom do the Scriptures testify?

_____

Where is life to be found?

_____

How does Jesus define eternal life in John 17:3?

_____

_____

According to 2 Corinthians 11:3, how are we led astray from our relationship with Christ?

_____

_____

I'm Ready to Listen to You

Many of the sermons we hear challenge us to do more, to be better Christians, or to make a difference in this world. I responded to a challenge to "Come Help Change the World." It sounded so good, but soon I realized I couldn't even change me.

Who will teach you all things, according to 1 John 2:27?

_____

_____

To whom does the Spirit testify, according to John 16:14?

_____

What does Colossians 2:21,22 say about the man-made commands we submit to?

_____

_____

What do these regulations have an appearance of, according to verse 23?

_____

_____

What are they unable to do?

_____

Where should we set our hearts and minds, according to Colossians 3:1,2?

_____

What does Galatians 5:22,23 say is the result of keeping our eyes on Christ?

_____

_____

Paul asked the Galatians, "What has happened to your joy?" He asks us the same question today.

Through error we have turned our relationship with Christ into a job. Maybe you are like me. I was committed to God's plan, but had strayed from the God of the plan.

I got tired of pretending. I wanted reality in my life. Finally, I pulled off the expressway and said to God, "I'm ready to listen to You."

Are you ready to listen to God? If so, know that what He will teach you is real, and that through His truth you will once again experience the joy of your salvation.

2

. . . .

The Truth
About Error

. . . .

I'm Going to Get You

One night I received a phone call from Pete. I had tried to help Pete in the past with his alcohol problems. He stopped seeing me, so I was surprised to get his call. Pete wanted me to do something for him I couldn't do. The more he tried to persuade me, the madder he got. Finally he shouted, "I'm going to get you!" and slammed down the phone.

Shortly after going to bed, I heard a loud noise outside. I looked out and saw Pete carrying a huge knife. After I secured my family, I went downstairs ready to clobber Pete with a baseball bat. Pete kicked down the front door, and with all the strength I could muster, I began swinging. I hit him again and again until I knew he was unconscious. I backed away, horrified at what I had done.

And all this happened that very night—in my mind. I experienced fear, my heart pounded, and my body was sweating and trembling with anger as I thought about defending my family. I experienced all these emotions while I was lying in my nice, warm bed.

Pete never came to my house that night. In fact, he was probably at home sound asleep. So, why did I feel emotionally as if he had come over? I'm sure you have had a similar experience. After you calm down you feel a little stupid, wondering why you got so scared. These experiences make us ask, "Why do we feel the way we do?"

Emotions and How They Work

The last time you were at a scary movie, did what you see and hear on the screen actually happen?

_____

Did your emotions know that what you saw was not real?

_____

What did your emotions respond to?

_____

Our emotions are responders. They *always* follow thought. They cannot distinguish fact from fantasy. Nor can they discern the difference between the past, present, and future.

That is why error is so dangerous. Whatever we put in our minds will determine how we feel.

If you are angry, jealous, afraid, or depressed, what kind of thoughts are you thinking?

_____

_____

What does Paul tell us to think on in Philippians 4:8?

_____

_____

Why?

_____

_____

The Truth About Error

Doreen was admitted into the hospital in a fetal position. She hadn't bathed herself or eaten a meal in days. Her physician called me to see if I could talk with Doreen. Doreen admitted that her depression had come from thinking about her daughter's wedding. Everything about the wedding was wrong.

We began to break the problem down point by point. I talked with Doreen from the premise truth sets you free; error binds you. My job that day was to identify the error in her mind and dispel it with the truth of God and His Word.

According to John 8:31,32, what was Doreen's problem?

_____

_____

Was Doreen's depression based on truth or error?

_____

What did Doreen need to be set free?

_____

_____

A Raging War

The war between truth and error began in the Garden of Eden. Satan convinced Eve to believe his lies instead of God's truth. Satan's goal today is to convince us that his lie is actually the truth.

Read Genesis 3:1-13.

How is Satan described in verse 1?

_____

What was God's command to Adam in Genesis 2:16,17?

_____

_____

How do Satan's statements to Eve in Genesis 3:1,4,5 compare to what God told Adam?

_____

_____

_____

Did Satan speak truth to Eve?

_____

How did Eve see the fruit of the tree after listening to Satan?

_____

_____

How did Adam and Eve respond to God after they had eaten of the tree, according to verses 8 and 10?

_____

_____

How does John 8:44 describe Satan?

_____

_____

Is there any truth in Satan?

_____

In Genesis 3:13, what was the reason Eve gave for eating the fruit?

_____

Satan deceived Eve, making her see the fruit as good for food, pleasing to the eye, and desirable for gaining wisdom. How does he convince us today to believe his lies?

_____

_____

Bank Teller Christianity

Bank tellers are trained to spot counterfeit money by being so familiar with the real thing that they can readily detect the imitation. Satan counterfeits God's truth. Our defense against Satan's lies is to become so familiar with truth as revealed by God in Scripture that, when we are confronted with error, it is easily discerned.

Satan Says

Who controls the ways of this world, according to Ephesians 2:2?

_____

The chart on the next page lists several lies that Satan tries to convince us to believe. Look up the Scriptures listed to compare what Satan says with what God says.

• • • • • • • • • • • • • • • • • •

Satan Says—Error	**God Says—Truth**
1. Seek success at any price.	Matthew 6:33 _____
	_____
	_____
2. Seek riches at any cost.	Matthew 6:19,20 _____
	_____
	_____
3. Be popular; push ahead.	Matthew 16:24 _____
	_____
	_____
4. Look out for number one.	Philippians 2:3,4 _____
	_____
	_____
5. You can't be happy until you're _____ (fill in the blank)	Philippians 4:11 _____
	_____
	_____
6. Eat, drink, and be merry.	Matthew 4:4 _____
	_____
	_____
7. If it feels good, do it.	Luke 22:42 _____
	_____
	_____
8. Everything is relative.	John 17:17 _____
	_____
	_____

• • • • • • • • • • • • • • • •

In Matthew 4:4, what does Jesus say that man needs to live?

_____

Where should we go for truth, according to John 17:17?

_____

Who Can Understand?

Many of us have had the experience of reading the Bible and not being able to understand its meaning. It just didn't make sense. We may have understood what it was saying, but we didn't have a clue as to what it meant. So how can we understand the Word of God?

I Know What You Are Thinking

According to 1 Corinthians 2:11, can you know the thoughts of another person?

_____

In the same way, can you know the thoughts of God?

_____

Who does 1 Corinthians 2:12 say that we have received?

_____

For what purpose?

_____

_____

Whose mind does verse 16 say we have?

_____

Whose responsibility is it to teach us the truth of God's Word and to explain to us those things God has freely given us?

_____

A Humble Heart

How are we to receive the Word of God, according to James 1:21?

_____

_____

What is the Word of God able to do?

_____

_____

In James 4:6, who does it say God gives grace to?

_____

As you continue working through this study guide, do so with an open, teachable heart. Many of the verses discussed may be familiar to you, but I pray you will see them with fresh eyes. Humbly listen to what God is saying. He wants to teach you truth that will set you free!

3

• • • • • • • • • • • • • • • • • •

Man Alive!
The Neglected Half
of the Gospel

• • • • • • • • • • • • • • • • • •

Nothing Seemed to Happen

Stan was drunk again. Sue, his wife, called me in the middle of the night to help out. I had talked to Stan numerous times about a relationship with Jesus Christ. He had always been very open to the gospel message. He had even walked an aisle to profess his faith in Christ, but nothing seemed to happen or change in his life. What was I going to say that night that would help?

I walked into the living room, and there was Stan— drunk, with that familiar empty expression. We covered much of the same territory we had discussed in previous conversations. Finally I asked something I had never asked before: "Stan, when you received Christ, which Jesus did you believe in? Did you receive Jesus the man, or Jesus the God, who is alive today, who offers to come and live inside you and give you His very life?"

Stan looked up at me intently, and said, "I received that Jesus who was a man 2000 years ago." That night

Stan accepted the living Christ. As I looked into his face, I saw a new man.

What's Your Understanding of the Gospel?

The Colossians had heard the gospel. In Colossians 1:6 what did Paul say this gospel was doing in the Colossians and all over the world?

_____

What does Colossians 1:6 say that the Colossians had heard and understood?

_____

Before Stan truly received Christ, he tried to imitate Jesus. Had he understood God's grace in all its truth?

_____

What did his insufficient understanding of the gospel produce in his life?

_____

_____

Paul reminded the Corinthians of the gospel he preached to them. What is that gospel, according to 1 Corinthians 15:3,4?

_____

_____

If a person's understanding of the gospel is nothing more than "Christ died for my sins," does he have an understanding of the gospel in all its truth?

_____

How much of the gospel are you functioning with?

_____

Does an understanding of only half the gospel—"Christ died for my sins"—give you the power to live and experience the abundant life here and now?

_____

Stan's story helped me see the missing link in my understanding of the gospel. I gladly accepted the forgiveness God provided at the cross, but that is where my understanding stopped. I had no clue as to what Christ's resurrection meant.

It Was There All the Time

What is the significance of the resurrection? My mind drew a blank for the first ten years of my Christian experience. Finally the obvious answer jumped out at me: Jesus Christ was raised from the dead, and resurrection is the restoration of LIFE!

I had missed the life of Christ. After that, it was like someone had rewritten the Bible. "Life" was everywhere.

According to Romans 5:10, how are we saved?

_____

_____

Why did Jesus say He came? See John 10:10.

_____

Based on John 5:24, what happens to us when we place our faith in Christ?

_____

John 3:16 is familiar to most of us. What does this verse say we receive when we believe in Christ?

_____

Jesus Christ said that He came to give life. The obvious question is "What kind of person needs life?"

From God's point of view, the problem of man is not just that he is a sinner in need of forgiveness; his greater problem is that he is dead and in need of life.

Dead Men Don't Need Help

Stan hated himself for what he had become through alcohol. With all the sincerity and willpower he could muster, he had tried to change. He had asked God to help him change. But something was missing.

Stan needed the very life of Christ. The night he received the living Christ, Stan changed. The difference I saw was the difference between a dead man and a living one.

How Did We Die?

How was man created, according to Genesis 1:27?

_____

What was God's command to Adam in Genesis 2:17?

_____

What did God say would happen to Adam the day he ate the fruit?

_____

What did Adam do in Genesis 3:6?

_____

Into whose likeness was Seth born, according to Genesis 5:3?

_____

According to Romans 5:12, how did sin enter the world?

_____

What was the result of Adam's sin?

_____

To how many men did death spread?

_____

In what condition were we born into this world, according to Ephesians 2:1?

_____

Sin entered the world through Adam, and as a result of sin came death. The day Adam ate the fruit, he forfeited his life in God. We are born into this world in the image of Adam—dead spiritually. And dead men don't need help; they need life.

The Neglected Half of the Gospel

How does Colossians 2:13 describe us before knowing Christ?

_____

What did God do for you and me?

_____

_____

How are we saved, according to Ephesians 2:8,9?

_____

_____

How does Paul define salvation in Ephesians 2:5?

_____

_____

Read 1 John 5:11-13.

Where is eternal life found?

_____

If you have the Son, what else do you have?

_____

Why did John write these things to us who believe on the name of the Son of God?

_____

_____

What is the real issue of salvation, according to these passages?

_____

_____

Who lives in you, according to Galatians 2:20?

_____

Whose responsibility is it to produce the Christian life in you?

_____

What is your responsibility?

_____

_____

What is our hope according to Colossians 1:27?

_____

_____

Salvation is the process of passing from death to life. It is not just something Christ did for you; it is Jesus Christ Himself living in you.

We can't live the Christian life—only Christ can. That is why Jesus Christ came not only to get men out of hell and into heaven, but also to get Himself out of heaven and into men.

Rejoice! Once you were dead, but now God has made you alive together with Christ. Christ in you is your only hope of glory.

4

• • • • • • • • • • • • • • • • • • •

Forgiven
to Be Filled

• • • • • • • • • • • • • • • • • • •

Take a Rest

Edward approached me after a seminar lecture and asked, "How can you know that God forgives your sins?" I had just spoken for over an hour on God's total forgiveness in Christ, so Edward's question surprised me.

Edward's struggle began as a child. He explained, "When I was young, I did something very wrong. Every day since then I have begged God to forgive me, but I just can't believe that He has."

I could hardly believe my ears. For more than 50 years, Edward had experienced nothing but fear and guilt, wondering if God could forgive a single past failure. He sadly admitted, "I should have been serving Him for those 50 years, but I have wasted my life."

What a tragedy! But Edward's story is not unique. Guilt over past sins keeps many of us from ever maturing as Christians. Because we refuse to settle the sin issue, many of us miss out on all that God has intended for us to experience through His indwelling life.

We learned in Chapter 3 that we have been made alive together with Christ, and that Christ lives in us. Christ laid down His life for us so that He could give His life to us. To experience the life of Christ in us, we must first learn to rest in Christ's death for us. Until we rest in the finality of the cross, we will never experience the reality of the resurrection.

Do You Need Glasses?

Peter says to those who are struggling with past sins and are not maturing that they have become nearsighted and blind. They need glasses to see that the sin issue between God and man is over. It's a variation on our theme: If truth sets you free, then error binds you.

Let's put on our glasses to see truth regarding the forgiveness issue.

Read 2 Peter 1:3-9.

How much have we been given pertaining to life and godliness? See verse 3.

_____

What have we become partakers of? See verse 4.

_____

What qualities are we to add to our faith? See verses 5-7.

_____

_____

What is the motivation to add to our faith the qualities mentioned in verses 5-7? See verses 3-5.

_____

Does a person attain these qualities overnight, or through the process of maturity? See verse 8.

_____

What will these qualities keep you from being? See verse 8.

_____

How does Peter describe someone who does not possess these qualities? See verse 9.

_____

What have they forgotten? See verse 9.

_____

Why did Edward waste 50 years of his life struggling with guilt, according to this passage?

_____

_____

How do Edward's life and this passage verify the statement, "Until you rest in the finality of the cross, you will never experience the reality of the resurrection?"

_____

_____

If you are struggling with guilt, wondering if God can forgive you, what does this passage say is the reason?

_____

Will You Stop Begging?

Edward begged God every day for over 50 years to forgive him. I asked Edward how it would make him feel if one of his kids doubted his forgiveness and asked him day after day, "Daddy, are you sure that you forgive me?"

Edward, with a pained expression, responded, "It would break my heart." Finally, the message was getting through. With fresh eyes, Edward was ready to look at the dozens of promises that teach that God has forgiven all our sins, once and for all.

How many times did Christ die for sins, according to 1 Peter 3:18?

_____

How many sins did He die for?

_____

What was the purpose of Christ's death?

_____

What did Christ come to do, according to John 1:29?

_____

What did God make Christ on our behalf, according to 2 Corinthians 5:21?

_____

Did Christ deserve to be made sin?

_____

What do we become in Christ?

_____

Did you earn righteousness or was it a free gift, according to Romans 5:17?

_____

If you have the righteousness of God in Christ, what can you conclude about the sin issue between you and God?

_____

_____

What does Ephesians 1:7 say we have in Christ?

_____

If you are in Christ, does it make much sense to beg God for something you already have?

_____

If you are resting in Christ's finished work on the cross concerning your sins, what will you be preoccupied with: sin or life?

_____

Based on the above verses, why do you think it is important to rest in the finality of the cross?

_____

_____

Edward finally got the message. At the end of our discussion, he asked if he could pray. His prayer went something like this:

> Lord Jesus, today I'm going to stop begging You to forgive me, and start trusting You for what You did for me on the cross. Now, from this day on, teach me what it means that You live in me.

Canning:
Cleansing, Filling and Sealing

Christ died for us then so He can live in us today. The process of canning further illustrates this point.

Let's say you are going to preserve some peaches. The first step is to sterilize the jars. Why? So that you can put the peaches in the jars without spoiling the fruit.

You cleanse the jars to put something in them. It wouldn't make much sense to cleanse the jars just for the sake of having clean jars around. But this is what we have done with the gospel. We have separated God's sterilization process from His filling process. In so doing, we have lost sight of the purpose of forgiveness. God had to deal with sin once and for all so that we could be filled with Christ "without spoiling."

Once and for All

What does Hebrews 8:10-12 say are the provisions of the New Covenant?

_____

_____

_____

When does a covenant go into effect, according to Hebrews 9:16,17?

_____

Why was it necessary for Jesus to die, according to Hebrews 9:22?

_____

Jesus had to die to usher in the New Covenant and to provide total forgiveness of sins.

Under the Old Covenant, the blood of bulls and goats was shed annually to cover the sins committed that year. These sacrifices did not cover future sins. A sacrifice had to be made the next year, and the next year, and the next. The sin issue was never over.

In contrast, Jesus offered Himself as one sacrifice for all time. The sin issue between God and man is over. Yet many of us, like Edward, live our lives under the old system, trying to cover our sins year after year.

Read Hebrews 10:1-18 and then answer the following questions.

How does the writer describe the law in verse 1?

_____

Can the law, through its annual sacrifices, make perfect those who draw near?

_____

If it could, would there be a need for further sacrifices, according to verse 2?

_____

Why?

_____

_____

Could the sacrifices the priest made again and again take away sins? See verse 11.

_____

How does verse 12 describe the sacrifice of Jesus?

_____

How is His sacrifice different from those sacrifices made under the Old Covenant?

_____

What did Christ do after He offered His sacrifice?

_____

What is the result of that one sacrifice made by Jesus for you and me? See verse 14.

_____

Since we have forgiveness of sins, is there any longer a need for a sacrifice for sin? See verse 18.

_____

If there were any more forgiveness needed for you and me, what would Christ have to do?

_____

_____

Based on the passages in this chapter, what is the purpose of forgiveness?

_____

_____

Why do you think it is important to settle the sin issue by resting in the finality of the cross?

_____

_____

_____

Christ said, "It is finished." Is it finished in your heart? If you are struggling with guilt, I pray that you, like Edward, will settle the sin issue once and for all.

5

. . . .

Putting the
Pieces Together

. . . .

The Big Picture

Have you ever tried to put together a jigsaw puzzle without the cover of the box? Without the big picture, it's hard to tell where the pieces fit in the puzzle.

In the last two chapters we have examined the "life and death" issue of salvation, and discovered that salvation is more than forgiveness of sins; it is receiving the life of Christ. The emphasis of the big picture is new life in Jesus Christ.

But how is this new life lived out? Questions like this usually follow when people are challenged to examine their understanding of the gospel. Perhaps you have grasped the big picture, but are wondering how some of the pieces fit.

The Wages of Sin Is...

During a seminar, Don raised his hand to ask a

question. "Bob, I've been taught that a Christian can lose his salvation. I know that Christ died for our past sins, but what about our future sins? I don't understand why Christ had to take away all sins."

Don's question revealed something about his understanding of the gospel. Don certainly did not want to lose his salvation, so all he could think of was how to get forgiveness when he sinned. Don's question sounds very familiar to us. We all sin and have wondered at times how we stand before God.

To answer Don's question, let's look again at the big picture of salvation. There we will discover why Christ had to take away all our sins.

What does Romans 6:23 say is the wages of sin?

_____

What do we deserve from God every time we sin?

_____

What did Christ become for you and me, according to 2 Corinthians 5:21?

_____

Since Christ knew no sin, whose sins did He die for?

_____

When Christ died for your sins, how many of them were in the future?

_____

First John 2:2 (alternate rendering) reads: "He is the one who turns aside God's wrath, taking away our sins, and not only ours but also the sins of the whole world."

On whom was God's wrath poured out?

_____

Who deserved God's wrath for sin?

_____

What has Christ done with our sins?

_____

What does Romans 3:25,26 say the cross demonstrates?

_____

According to these verses, what does God do for those who have faith in Jesus?

_____

_____

If Christ took all the punishment and the entire wrath of God for our sins, how much punishment and wrath is left for you and me?

_____

_____

The Gift of God Is...

We have already learned that the real issue of salvation is raising dead men to life. Christ turned aside God's wrath for you and me by taking away our sins. If He had not done so, we would never be able to experience the life of Christ.

Let's imagine that someone has died of cancer. If you had the power to save this person, how many problems would you have to solve? Two! You would have to raise him to life, but you would also have to cure his cancer.

If you cured just the cancer, the man might be healthy, but he would remain dead. If you raised him to life without curing the cancer, he would simply die again.

This is a perfect picture of the condition of man. Sin entered the world through Adam, and as a result, death, and death spread to all men. So that man could truly experience *eternal* life, God had to cure the disease that killed man: sin.

What is the gift of God according to Romans 6:23?

_____

If the death of Christ had not turned aside the wrath of God and taken away our sins, what would happen to us each time we sinned?

_____

_____

Adam was created spiritually alive. According to Romans 5:12, what caused Adam to die?

_____

_____

For whose sin did Jesus die, according to 2 Corinthians 5:21?

_____

How can you and I know that we will never die spiritually again, even though we still commit sins as Christians?

_____

_____

God has completely dealt with our sin at the cross. The disease that killed us has been cured, and we can know that our salvation is secure forever.

God's Search for Man

Sometimes it is not that our understanding of salvation is wrong; it is just too small. God uses many words to describe the completeness of our salvation. One such word that expresses the finality of the sin issue is "reconciliation."

According to 2 Corinthians 5:18,19, how did Christ reconcile us to Himself?

_____

Upon whose initiative was the world reconciled to God?

_____

What is the ministry that God has committed to us?

_____

How many things did Christ reconcile to Himself, according to Colossians 1:20?

_____

Why did God reconcile you through Christ's death, according to Colossians 1:22?

_____

What do you think is the purpose of reconciliation, based on Colossians 1:27?

_____

_____

The entire world has been reconciled to God through the cross, but reconciliation alone is not salvation. Reconciliation means that the barrier between God and man has been taken away, and a bridge has been built between the two through the person of Jesus Christ. The reason that God has removed the sin barrier is so that whosoever will come to Christ by faith can be made alive in Him. That is why the only thing that will ever condemn a man to hell is simply his refusal to accept life.

The Life of a New Creation

All this emphasis on total forgiveness and Christ living in you threatens many people. They picture lazy people sitting around, waiting for something to happen. Of course, this could not be further from the truth.

Let me share an illustration that might help. Let's imagine that a king issued a blanket pardon to all the prostitutes in his land. If you were a prostitute, that would be good news. No longer would you have to live in hiding, but would this decree give you any motivation to change your lifestyle?

Let's take the illustration further. Suppose the king asked one of the prostitutes to become his bride. What happens when a prostitute marries a king? She becomes a queen. Would her new identity as queen motivate her to change her lifestyle? It wouldn't make much sense for the queen to go back to her former lifestyle, would it?

The motivation for you and me to change is the fact that we are the bride of Christ. We have a brand-new identity.

What does 2 Corinthians 5:17 say we have become?

_____

What has happened to the old things?

_____

What does Ephesians 5:8 say that we once were?

_____

What are we now?

_____

Because we are children of light, how should we live?

_____

_____

Do we always act as new creatures in Christ?

_____

Does how we act determine our identity if we are in Christ?

_____

According to Colossians 3:1-3, whose perspective should we adopt to determine our true identity?

_____

_____

Salvation is our being made a new creation, like a caterpillar becoming a butterfly. We were once sinners, but through spiritual birth God has transformed us into saints. We have a brand-new identity. We may do sinful things, but we will never be sinners again—just like the butterfly may crawl around with the worms, but it will never be a worm again.

6

....

Toward a
Proper Self-image

....

Who Are You?

Our identity is determined by who or what we are identified with. Imagine living on a deserted island without ever having human contact. If a voice from heaven asked, "Who are you?" you wouldn't have the slightest clue how to answer. If someone suddenly appeared and said, "I'm John Doe, and you are my child, Pat," then you would have an identity. If the voice from heaven asked again, "Who are you?" you would respond, "I'm Pat Doe, John Doe's child."

Discovering who we are is a basic need of every human heart. In our desperate attempts to discover our identity, we will latch onto practically anything to be able to finally say, "This is who I am."

List some ways that we try to determine our identity apart from Christ.

_____

What happens to our identity if we depend on the opinion of others to determine who we are?

_____

_____

Do the opinions of others ever change?

_____

What does Matthew 7:26,27 say happens to the house built on sand when the storms come?

_____

If we determine our identity through temporal things, such as our profession, our appearance, or the opinions of others, what will happen to us when the storms of life come?

_____

_____

A Firm Foundation

Jimmy walked into my office for a counseling appointment. Before we started, he said, "By the way, I am a paranoid, manic-depressive schizophrenic." What a marvelous self-image! But that is how Jimmy had seen himself through most of his adult life.

If your identity is a paranoid, manic-depressive schizophrenic, the most natural way to act is like a paranoid, manic-depressive schizophrenic. But God has given you a new identity. If you are in Christ, you are a child of God!

What is our identity, according to Galatians 3:26?

_____

How do we become sons of God?

_____

Do we become sons of God by what we do, or by who we believe in?

_____

According to Galatians 4:6, because we are sons, who did God send into our hearts?

_____

What does God's Spirit cry out?

_____

In 1 John 2:1, what is our identity even when we sin?

_____

Because we are sons, even if we have sinned, how should we approach the throne of grace, according to Hebrews 4:16?

_____

Because we have placed our faith in Jesus Christ, we are children of God. That is our new identity. Jimmy was not a paranoid, manic-depressive schizophrenic. He was and is a child of God. I am not Bob George, a criticizaholic. I am a child of God. And so are you, if you are in Christ. God has given us the right to be His children. Because we are sons, we can approach God without fear.

Only Two Kinds of People

We have already stated that our identity comes from who or what we are identified with. In this world there are all types of people with all types of different labels attached, but from God's vantage point there are only two kinds of people in this world: those who are in Adam, and those who are in Christ.

To "be in" somebody may sound strange to you. But to be in someone means that he is our family head. As such, he has left us his name, his nature, an inheritance, and a destiny. The two family heads in this world are Adam and Jesus Christ. They determine who we are, our nature, our inheritance, and our destiny. And the two stand in total contrast to each other.

How God Changes Your Identity

As a boy, I used to play ball with my dog, Rusty. Rusty was a good retriever, but occasionally he would lose sight of the ball. I tried to help him find it by pointing my finger to where the ball was, but to no avail. Rusty found my finger more interesting.

That is the way we are with God. Instead of catching on to what God really wants us to know, we focus on God's symbols, or pointing fingers. Baptism is one of these symbols.

The word "baptize" was used to describe the process of dyeing. To change the color of a white piece of cloth, you would place it into a vat of red dye. When you pulled it out, you had a red piece of cloth. The cloth was totally identified with what it had been placed in.

The key meaning behind baptism is total identification. Through baptism, God changes our identity by placing us in Christ.

What does 1 Corinthians 15:22 say about those in Adam?

_____

_____

What does this verse say about those in Christ?

_____

_____

How are we born into this world, according to Ephesians 2:1?

_____

From Romans 5:15-19 list the consequences of being in Adam.

_____

_____

From these same verses list the consequences of being in Christ.

_____

_____

How are we placed into the body of Christ, according to 1 Corinthians 12:13?

_____

_____

Who does Galatians 3:27 say we have clothed ourselves with if we have been baptized into Christ?

_____

_____

When God sees us, who does He see?

_____

What is the result of being baptized into Christ, according to Romans 6:4?

_____

_____

What have we become in Christ, according to 2 Corinthians 5:17?

_____

Through spiritual baptism, God has changed our identity. In Adam, I was Bob George without God's Spirit, spiritually dead, a guilty sinner. Galatians 2:20 tells me that I have been crucified with Christ. That old person is dead and gone. Today, I am a new creation in Christ. I am Bob George with God's Spirit living in me, spiritually alive, and totally forgiven.

You, too, are a new creation in Christ—not because of what you do, but because God has placed you into His Son.

A Proper Self-Image

Janet had been hospitalized for several weeks for anorexia and bulimia. She had been so obsessed with her weight that she had almost literally starved herself to death. Her doctors told her that her problem was low self-esteem. They had Janet practicing a Hindu meditation technique of "catching the sunlight and bringing it into your body" to restore her health, strength, and self-confidence.

Janet underwent this type of treatment for six weeks with no results. After the six weeks, her parents brought her to our ministry. Janet's problem was not a poor self-image. In fact, Janet was totally preoccupied with Janet—what she looked like and what others thought about her. She didn't need a "positive" self-image. She needed a proper self-image, based on truth.

How does 2 Timothy 3:2 describe what people will be like during the end times?

_____

_____

Does this description match what we see daily in the headlines and on TV?

_____

Is our problem low self-esteem like the world tells us, or is it that we love ourselves too much?

_____

What does Romans 12:3 warn us about?

_____

_____

How should we think of ourselves?

_____

_____

How does God see us, according to Ephesians 1:4-7?

_____

_____

According to 1 Corinthians 1:30,31, who placed us in Christ?

_____

What has Christ Jesus become for us?

_____

_____

Does this leave any room for boasting on our part?

_____

What should our attitude be, according to Philippians 2:3?

_____

_____

What did Christ come to do, according to Matthew 20:28?

_____

If Christ lives in you, what will He be teaching you to do?

_____

_____

In Christ we are children of God. We are loved perfectly, accepted totally, and seen as perfect in God's eyes. This is our identity in Christ. Within a week of understanding her identity in Christ, Janet became free of her destructive behavior. When we grasp who we are, we will go free. We will be free to serve others and to look after other people's interests, not just our own. There we will find true meaning and purpose to life.

7

. . . .

Loved *and*
Accepted

. . . .

I Know You Love Me, But...

My son, Bobby, had just graduated from college. The economy was down in Dallas, and he was having a difficult time landing his first job. Bobby was getting down on himself and needed a little encouragement. I invited him to breakfast to see if I could offer him some encouragement and advice.

During the discussion, Bobby seemed to perk up. We talked about work, the business world, interviewing, and then we went on to talk about other things. We enjoyed a good time of just being together. As our conversation was winding down, Bobby said, "Dad, one thing I've always known is that you love me. I have never doubted it. You've shown me in all kinds of ways."

I appreciated what he said, but somehow it didn't seem complete. I was silent for a few seconds, then God seemed to put a new thought in my mind. "Bobby," I said, "I really do love you, but let me ask you a question. Have you always known that I *accept* you? Do you know that I accept you just the way you are—that I really like *you*?"

Bobby thought for awhile and then answered, "No, Dad, I don't think I have really felt that you accept me." Many Christians are like Bobby. They know God loves them, but deep down in their hearts they have never believed that God truly accepts them just for who they are. How would you answer if God asked you, "Do you know that I accept you?"

The Phantom Christian

The Phantom Christian is that imaginary person who many of us are continually comparing ourselves to. He is the one who can do no wrong. He never gets angry or has a bad thought; he loves everyone. He gets up early each morning to pray and study the Bible. He is totally engrossed in church activities throughout the week. He is tops in his field at work. And on top of all that, he is a sterling example of a loving husband and a devoted father.

Who could live up to such a standard? Yet in the back of our minds we think the Phantom Christian is God's standard of acceptance. With every bad thought or missed quiet time, God's acceptance of us slips further and further away. As a result, we live our lives under continual guilt, with God seemingly a million miles away.

If you are trying to live up to the standard of the Phantom Christian or to God's law, what does Galatians 3:10 say you are under?

_____

_____

Why?

_____

_____

Could anyone ever live up to "everything written in the Book of the Law"?

_____

Could anyone ever live up to the standards of the Phantom Christian?

_____

How do we act toward God when we fear we have not pleased Him by living up to His standards?

_____

_____

How should we approach God in our time of need, according to Hebrews 4:16?

_____

Ephesians 1:6 (KJV) reads: "To the praise of the glory of his grace, wherein he hath made us accepted in the beloved."

What are we made in the Beloved?

_____

Where is our acceptance found?

_____

Who made us accepted in the Beloved?

_____

Is God's grace something we earn, or is it a free gift, according to Ephesians 2:8,9?

_____

Could we ever earn God's acceptance through our own efforts?

_____

If you are in Christ, how accepted are you?

_____

Get rid of the Phantom Christian in your mind. He is not real. All of us blow it and fall flat on our faces continually. But even when we fall flat on our faces, because we are in Christ, God accepts us. He made us acceptable!

Will You Raise Your Hand?

I was speaking on the subject of our identity in Christ to the student body of a seminary. To make a point, I asked, "How many of you are as righteous and acceptable in the sight of God as Jesus Christ?" Only three hands went up.

How would you answer the question? Would you have raised your hand?

According to 2 Corinthians 5:21, what did God make Christ?

_____

What did He make you and me?

_____

If we are totally righteous, how acceptable are we in God's sight?

_____

How was Abraham made righteous, according to Romans 4:3?

_____

How does Romans 3:22 say the righteousness of God comes to you and me?

_____

According to Galatians 3:24, how are we justified (declared totally righteous)?

_____

What does God say about the wicked in 1 Corinthians 6:9?

_____

Who does Romans 4:5 say God justifies?

_____

_____

What does 1 Corinthians 6:9-11 say we once were?

_____

_____

What has happened to us?

_____

_____

Are you as righteous and acceptable in the sight of God as Jesus Christ?

_____

_____

My son, Bobby, knew that I loved him. He didn't know that I accepted him, that I really liked him just for who he was. He believed in his heart that he was not living up to my standards, that I disapproved of him. As the years went by, he became more and more distant from me. That's the way we are with God.

We know that He loves us, but that becomes practically meaningless in our daily lives because we believe He doesn't accept us. The truth is that God sees us as totally acceptable and righteous in His sight right now— not because of what we do, because of what Christ has done for us.

Do You Really Believe?

If you really believed deep down in your heart that you were as righteous as Jesus Christ, how would that belief change your attitudes toward God and other people? It would make a difference, wouldn't it?

The first application where we will discover whether or not we really believe we are as righteous as Jesus is prayer. How we pray reveals our perception of God's acceptance and what we think He desires from us.

According to Hebrews 4:16, how are we to approach God?

_____

When does this verse say we should approach Him?

_____

When is your greatest time of need?

_____

_____

_____

When you have fallen flat on your face, or you are experiencing temptation, or you are caught in the grip of some sin, what do you naturally expect from God?

_____

_____

What does this verse say you will receive from God?

_____

How do we boldly and confidently approach God, according to Ephesians 3:12?

_____

How are we to pray, according to John 14:14?

_____

What do you think it means to pray in Jesus' name?

_____

_____

Apart from Christ and His righteousness, are we acceptable to God?

_____

Whose righteousness must we stand in to boldly and confidently approach God?

_____

Who are we clothed in, according to Galatians 3:27?

_____

How acceptable are we to God if we are clothed with Christ?

_____

Standing in Christ's righteousness, what assurance do we have in approaching God, according to 1 John 5:14,15?

_____

_____

Is this good news?

_____

Do you really believe it?

_____

Prayer is the key application of our identity in Christ because it is inescapable. The Bible tells us to "pray continually," and that is our heart's desire. It is because we have been made righteous and acceptable that we have assurance in approaching Him, that in whatever we ask, He hears us. Because of who we are, when we go to God we will find grace and mercy in our time of need.

8

· · · · · · · · · · · · · · · · · ·

The Great
Exchange

· · · · · · · · · · · · · · · · · ·

The Exchanged Life

Mr. Yates raised sheep on a huge tract of land in west Texas during the depression years. He lived in extreme poverty, struggling just to feed and clothe his family. He couldn't pay the small amount of taxes due on the land, and was in danger of losing his property. As Mr. Yates was facing inevitable bankruptcy, an oil company approached him. "There may be oil on your property," they said. "Will you allow us to drill?"

The oil company began drilling and struck the largest oil deposit at the time on the North American continent. The deposit produced over 80,000 barrels of oil every day. Overnight, Mr. Yates became a billionaire! Or did he? Mr. Yates had been a billionaire ever since he first acquired the land. The oil was always there. He just didn't know it!

Like Mr. Yates, most of us are unaware of the incredible riches that we *already have* in Christ. We live our

Christian lives in spiritual poverty, struggling just to make it day to day. But it doesn't have to be that way. There is oil on our property. In Christ, we have riches far greater than Mr. Yates'. God has blessed us with *every* spiritual blessing.

Are Your Eyes Open?

Many of the verses in this chapter will be familiar to you. They were to me. I used to teach these same verses years ago. But I can tell you for a fact that I didn't understand what I was talking about. These verses were all in my head, but not in my heart. And I learned that head knowledge doesn't help much when you're driving down the expressway with tears streaming down your cheeks, wondering "what went wrong."

Paul prayed in Ephesians that the "eyes of our hearts" would be opened. That's what I needed: a true heart knowledge of God and His love for me. My head knowledge was not enough; it didn't make sense. Today, my experience of God's love and acceptance is so real it's hard to describe. Are the "eyes of your heart" open to see what God has freely given you?

In 1 Corinthians 2:9, what does God say about those things He has prepared for those who love Him?

_____

_____

_____

How does Jesus describe the eyesight and hearing of the people to His disciples in Matthew 13:13-15?

_____

_____

What reason did He give for them not being able to perceive or understand?

_____

_____

In Matthew 13:16, why does Jesus say the disciples are blessed?

_____

_____

Why were the disciples able to hear and see, according to Matthew 13:11?

_____

Based on the above verses, are we able to perceive and understand the things God has prepared for us through our intellects or through our five senses?

_____

How can we learn and know about the things God has prepared for us, according to 1 Corinthians 2:10?

_____

Why has God given us the Holy Spirit, according to 1 Corinthians 2:12?

_____

In Ephesians 3, Paul prays that we will be strengthened with power through God's Spirit. According to verses 18-19, why do we need power?

_____

_____

What is the result of grasping hold of the love of God?

_____

Why does Paul pray that the "eyes of your heart may be enlightened" in Ephesians 1:18,19?

_____

_____

My life has been changed through these truths. It wasn't that God's truth had changed; rather, my understanding of His truth changed. I finally understood in my heart. It takes God's power for us to understand. That's why we must approach God's truth with a humble, teachable, dependent attitude.

You Are a Billionaire!

We have already learned in previous chapters that in Christ we are "heirs of God—coheirs with Christ." But what is our inheritance, and how does knowing this translate into a changed life? The principle that ties the two together is that *you will never have a changed life until you have experienced the exchanged life.*

Can you imagine the dramatic way becoming a billionaire overnight changed Mr. Yates' lifestyle? But this did not come about until he exchanged his poverty for the riches of the land. So it is with you and me. God did not call us to change our lives, but to experience the *exchanged* life. We give Christ all that we are—spiritually dead, guilty sinners—and Christ gives us all that He is—resurrected life, forgiveness, righteousness, acceptance. Our inheritance is the result of exchanging our identity. Let's go on now to examine all that we have in Christ.

According to Romans 5:1, what is the result of being justified through faith?

_____

Since we have been justified (declared totally righteous) what are we saved from, according to Romans 5:9,10?

_____

What were we when God reconciled us to Himself through the death of His Son?

_____

What do you think the phrase "how much more" means in these two verses?

_____

_____

Based on these verses, how can you be sure that God will not deal with you in anger because of your sins?

_____

_____

What is the result of being in Christ, according to Romans 8:1?

_____

Based on this verse, will you ever face judgment for your sins?

_____

What does Hebrews 10:14 say about you?

_____

Did you become perfect by what you did, or by what Jesus did?

_____

What have we been given in Christ, according to Colossians 2:9,10?

_____

Can you add to completeness?

_____

According to 2 Peter 1:3, do you need anything else for life and godliness?

_____

Does being complete mean that you are totally mature?

_____

On what can we rest confidently concerning our Christian maturity, according to Philippians 1:6?

_____

Where is our citizenship, according to Philippians 3:20?

_____

Whose ways did we follow when we were in Adam, according to Ephesians 2:1?

_____

In Christ Jesus, what are we created to do, according to Ephesians 2:10?

_____

Who prepared these good works for us?

_____

_____

When we realize the great love God has for us, how does this make us respond back to God, according to 1 John 4:19?

_____

_____

Because we have experienced God's great exchange, what are we free to concentrate on, according to Romans 6:4?

_____

_____

We truly are billionaires in Christ. The New Testament is so bold in its proclamation of the riches we have in Christ that it boggles the mind. Sometimes it is hard to believe that the Bible really means what it says. We do have peace with God, we are saved from His wrath, we are perfect forever in His sight—these are all true right now! Not because of the way we act, but because of what God has done through Jesus Christ. Through Christ, God has lavished the riches of His grace on us.

God's Power

Paul wrote in Roman 1:16, "I am not ashamed of the gospel, because it is the power of God for the salvation of everyone who believes. . . ." The gospel is a message of love, acceptance, and life. But this is not only so that we can go to heaven when we die. It is also the power of God for living here and now.

Many people look at our inheritance in Christ as just pie in the sky. They are thankful for what God has done, but it has little relevance here and now. They always want to go on to practical truth. The fact is that there is nothing more practical than the message of God's love and grace, and the believer's identity in Christ. People are always looking for God's power, and this is it.

You Are Not What You Do

Let's take a tough situation. Suppose someone who is caught up in homosexuality comes to you for counsel. Does Jesus Christ have an answer for him? Is the gospel truly the power of God that can change his life?

We all know homosexuality is wrong. The world can call it "sickness," an "alternative lifestyle," or a "sexual preference." But the Bible calls it sin. The answer, though, is not simply accepting homosexuality as sin or proving that it is wrong. What answer can we offer a man caught in this terrible bondage? I know of only one: He needs not just a change of behavior, but also a totally new identity.

Lee slumped in a chair in my office as he told his story. "I have been a homosexual for many years. Just a few months ago, I was introduced to Christ by some friends. I thought everything had changed, but now there is this guy at the church I'm attracted to and . . ." Lee continued to say that in spite of his efforts to change, he found himself falling back into the same old habits. How do we help Lee?

How did Lee identify himself at the beginning of the conversation?

What does 1 Corinthians 6:9,10 say about homosexual offenders?

If you were a homosexual offender (or anything else listed in the above verses), how would you feel knowing that homosexual offenders will not inherit the kingdom of God?

_____

_____

Lee identified himself as a homosexual. If he is in Christ, is that his identity according to God?

_____

What does God say about Lee, according to 1 Corinthians 6:11?

_____

_____

How did his identity change: by what he did or by what Christ did?

_____

How righteous was Lee the minute he accepted Christ, according to 2 Corinthians 5:21?

_____

How righteous was Lee when he was later tempted and fell back into his old habits?

_____

Even after Lee came to Christ, how did he identify himself: by his actions or by what God had done for him?

_____

_____

How does God identify Lee: by his actions or by what He has done for Lee?

_____

_____

Is our identity in Christ determined by what we do or by what Christ did?

_____

Do you think knowing how God sees you in the midst of your behavior provides hope and a motivation to change?

_____

It Doesn't Make Sense

Lee responded to our discussion of his identity in Christ this way: "Bob, if these things are who I really am, then that old activity just doesn't make any sense." That is the whole point. If your identity is that you're a child of God—holy, righteous, acceptable in His sight, then that old behavior makes no sense at all. It is totally inconsistent with who you are! Lee caught the truth, and it was the beginning of his turnaround.

Are the temptations we face common to man, according to 1 Corinthians 10:13?

_____

What must we trust when we're in the midst of our temptations?

_____

What will God provide for you when you are tempted?

_____

What does Paul tell us to do when we are tempted, according to Galatians 5:16?

_____

Does this verse say our desires or temptations will go away?

_____

What is the result of walking by the Spirit?

_____

What have we become, according to Ephesians 5:8?

_____

Because of who we are, how should we live?

_____

_____

Does this make sense?

_____

I have seen Lee and many others like him go free from a terrible bondage through learning their identity in Christ. Lee had to exchange an identity based on his behavior for an identity based on God's truth. Lee needed to recognize that at the moment he was born again, he had given Jesus all that he was and had received in return all that Christ is. In light of his new identity in Christ, Lee's old lifestyle just didn't make sense. Lee was now free to say no to sin and to say yes to the Lord Jesus Christ.

Whatever you or I may be struggling with, the answer is the same. It is only through a total exchange that we will begin to see the changes we desire.

9

. . . .

The Ministry
of Condemnation

. . . .

The Christian Life Is Killing Me!

Let's go now to Louisville, Kentucky. Marge, you're on 'People to People.'"

Marge in a quiet voice said, "I just want to ask if it's possible for a Christian to commit suicide and still go to heaven."

Marge wasn't asking out of mere curiosity. She was considering taking her own life. But how can a Christian get so deep in the pits? We have discussed the answer from several angles: Truth sets you free; therefore it is error that binds you. But what error could be causing Marge such pain?

Marge had been a Christian for about six years. Her early years in Christ were filled with joy and enthusiasm. She immersed herself in her church and, in her own words, was there "every time the doors opened."

The emphasis in her church was on "victory," with an attitude that "you and Jesus can defeat anything." "The only problem," Marge explained, "was that it wasn't working for me. I would go to church and get all pumped up, but at home and work I was down in the dumps. My life was like a roller coaster." Marge tried to do all the right things, but her problems continued.

Marge's cyclical pattern of work, failure, and depression deepened to the point where, she said, "I was ready to put a gun to my head. Since I was afraid to kill myself, I prayed every night to God that I wouldn't wake up in the morning. Since He hated me so much, I couldn't see any reason why He wouldn't at least answer that prayer."

Marge's story is a tragedy, but I find that most Christians are tangled up in the same error to some extent. I experienced her bondage and, as a matter of fact, this error has plagued the church for almost 2000 years. Much of the New Testament is devoted to this subject of law and grace.

The Issue of God's Acceptance

Law and grace is something we live every day, whether we know it or not. It involves how we approach our entire Christian lives, and the effects are far-reaching and profound. In the simplest of terms *law and grace is the issue of God's acceptance.* How are you and I made acceptable to God?

Marge's story is a perfect picture of someone mingling law and grace. Although she knew she was saved by grace through faith, she lived her Christian life trying to earn God's favor, trying to do enough to get God to deliver her from her problems. And this is where much of the Christian world lives today.

How are we saved, according to Ephesians 2:8,9?

Is our salvation a result of our works, or a free gift from God?

_____

We receive Christ by faith. According to Colossians 2:6, how are we to live in Him?

_____

_____

What is God's commandment for you and me in 1 John 3:23?

_____

_____

According to these verses, how should we live our lives as Christians?

_____

_____

What does Paul say about those who work, according to Romans 4:4?

_____

_____

According to Romans 4:2, if Abraham was justified by works, would he have something to boast about?

_____

If Abraham was justified by his works, what would he boast about: what he did or what God did?

_____

With works, where is the emphasis: on man or God?

_____

What does Paul contrast works with, in Romans 4:5?

_____

_____

What is the focus of faith: on what man does or on what God does?

_____

_____

What is the result of believing in Him who justifies the ungodly?

_____

_____

Where was the emphasis in Marge's life: on what Marge did for God, or on what God had done for her?

_____

Was Marge living by faith or works?

_____

What did she think God felt about her as a result?

_____

_____

Could Marge or anyone else ever be justified by the works of the law, according to Romans 3:20?

_____

Like Marge, people are attracted to Christ by the message of salvation by grace, but once they are in the family of God, they are leveled by demands for performance and conformity. But the Bible says that we can't have it both ways. "And if by grace, then it is no longer by works; if it were, grace would no longer be grace" (Romans 11:6).

You Foolish Galatians!

After Paul visited the province of Galatia and established the new believers in their faith, people called Judaizers came in behind him to "help" the new believers in their understanding of the gospel. These Judaizers preached that to be acceptable to God these new believers needed to be circumcised, observe the Sabbath, and follow the dietary commands of the law. They mingled law and grace.

Read Galatians 3:1-5.

What did Paul say in verse 1 had happened to the Galatians?

_____

What had been portrayed before their very eyes?

_____

_____

How did the Galatians receive the Spirit of God: through observing the law or by believing what they heard?

_____

What is the message of the cross to Christians, according to 1 Corinthians 1:18?

_____

In Romans 1:16 what does Paul say the gospel is and does for those who believe?

_____

_____

How does our human effort to attain salvation compare to the work of Jesus Christ?

_____

_____

In 1 Peter 1:9, how does Peter say we receive the goal of salvation?

_____

_____

What were the Galatians trying to attain through their human efforts, according to Galatians 3:3?

_____

If righteousness could be gained through the law, what would we have to say about Christ's death, according to Galatians 2:21?

_____

Why then do we have to rely on the grace of God?

_____

_____

We foolish Christians! We are just like the Galatians. We, too, are trying to attain our goal through human effort. If we could gain the righteousness of God through our human efforts, then Christ died for nothing. But His death and resurrection, the gospel, is the power of God for salvation. Our human efforts cannot compare to His work for you and me on the cross. Rest in the grace of God. It is through His efforts—not ours—that we are made acceptable in the sight of God.

The Ministry of Condemnation

Paul tells us in Romans that the law is good. We would all agree that trying to live up to the Ten Commandments is a good and noble goal. Yet, when we try to live up to the commandments, we feel guilty and condemned. Why?

We persist in bringing the law into our Christian lives because we have not come to grips with its real meaning and purpose. The law is a reflection of God's righteousness—not ours. And as we have already learned, we can never attain the righteousness of God through our obedience to the law. No matter how hard we try, our righteousness is as "filthy rags" in comparison to God's. So, why the law?

What Does the Mirror Show You?

The most important purpose of the law is in leading men to salvation. The law is like a mirror. A mirror shows you that your face is dirty, but it cannot wash it for you. The law, in the same way, shows us our sinfulness, but it cannot make us right before God. Let's look into the mirror of the law and find out what it shows us about ourselves.

In Romans 4:15, what does it say the law brings about?

_____

If there was no law, could there be a violation of the law?

_____

So what does the law define?

_____

_____

According to Romans 5:12,13, when did sin enter the world?

_____

Was sin in the world before the law came?

_____

What do we become conscious of through the law, according to Romans 3:19,20?

_____

What does James 2:10 say about those that stumble in just one point of the law?

_____

According to this verse, what is God's standard under law?

_____

Read Galatians 3:10.

What are those people who rely on observing the law under?

_____

How much of the law must you keep in order to avoid its curse?

_____

What is God's standard of acceptance under law?

_____

Can anybody live up to this standard?

_____

What do you think God is trying to show you through the law?

_____

_____

If this is not enough, Jesus Christ in His teaching ministry went beyond the written law to the spirit of the law. He magnified the demands of the law to include what goes on in the heart.

According to Matthew 5:21,22, what does the law say makes a person subject to judgment?

_____

What did Jesus say would bring about judgment?

_____

What is God's standard of acceptance under law—not only externally, but also in the heart, according to Matthew 5:48?

_____

How does Paul describe the law in verses 7 and 9 of 2 Corinthians 3?

_____

_____

What was the real cause of our death, according to Romans 7:13?

_____

Trying to live up to the law shows us our sinfulness and brings about condemnation and death. What is the only thing we can cry out to God if the law has truly done its work in our lives?

_____

_____

Read Galatians 3:21-24.

Can the law impart life?

_____

If it could, then what would righteousness be based on?

_____

_____

What does Scripture declare about the whole world?

_____

_____

Who is the promise given to?

_____

Before faith came, what held us prisoners?

_____

What was the law put in charge to do?

_____

If the law has pointed us to Christ so that we are justified by faith, does it have any further role to play in our lives?

What does Galatians 3:25 say about the need for the law now that faith has come?

Why did God give a law that would kill and condemn? He did it to kill and condemn. When the law brings about condemnation and death, it is doing its job. That is what it is supposed to do. Because God is cruel? No! Because it is a necessary ministry to bring us to salvation given through Jesus Christ. And that is God's desire: "This is good, and pleases God our Savior, who wants all men to be saved and to come to a knowledge of the truth" (1 Timothy 2:3,4).

The New Wineskins

Often the question is asked, "Aren't we still supposed to keep the Ten Commandments?" That is a good question. Right and wrong are still right and wrong. The law still is a reflection of God's character, and He never changes.

However, the Ten Commandments are not just "Thou shalt not murder." Attached to the commandment is a penalty if you do murder. You cannot separate the law from the penalty of the law. That is why, as we have already learned, those who are under the law are under a curse.

But God has something much better for us. He has called us to a life of faith so that we can experience the abundant life He promised. And this new life cannot be contained in the old wineskin called the law.

Under the law, what are the wages of sin, according to Romans 6:23?

_____

What does Romans 3:23 say that all people have done?

_____

_____

What has the law of the Spirit of life set you free from, according to Romans 8:2?

_____

According to Matthew 9:17, what happens when you pour new wine into old wineskins?

_____

_____

What is the result of pouring new wine into new wineskins?

_____

Based on this verse, can you mix law and grace?

_____

What do you think would happen if you did?

_____

_____

Who does Romans 10:4 say is the end of the law for us as believers?

_____

What are we now living under, according to Romans 6:14?

How does Paul contrast living under grace to living under the ministry of condemnation in Romans 8:1,2?

Like pouring new wine into old wineskins, when you mix law and grace, both are ruined. Law is robbed of its terror, and grace is robbed of its freedom and joy. The law has a purpose in our lives: to show us our sinfulness so that we will turn to Christ by faith. Once it has done its work, we are no longer under law, but under grace.

The law kills and condemns. That is exactly what it is supposed to do, so that we can receive new life in Jesus Christ.

10

Free from the Yoke of Slavery

The Banquet Table or the Garbage Can?

You are no longer under the law, but under grace." Many object, believing that this message will cause people to sin more. They say, "You're giving people a license to sin." These objections are not new. Paul dealt with them in his Epistle to the Romans. I hear these objections all the time, and I like to answer with an illustration.

Imagine that you own a fine cafeteria. One day you find in your garbage dumpsters a skeleton of a man rummaging for food. Moved with compassion, you say to him, "I want you to eat in my cafeteria from now on, free of charge. You can eat anything you want!"

"You really mean I can eat anything I want?"

"Yes, I said anything you want."

What would you think of this man if, after telling him he could eat anything he wanted, he asked, "Can I eat some garbage?" You would think he was insane. How absurd! Yet, we ask the same thing of God.

Jesus Christ laid down His life to set us free from the bondage of sin and death. He was raised from the dead so that we could have new life—Jesus Christ living in us and through us each and every day. And in the face of a "cafeteria line" like this, that Jesus called "abundant" life, all we can ask is, "Does that mean that you can just go out and sin more?" Somewhere along the way, we have missed the real goal of the Christian life.

Stay Out of the Garbage

The Christian world is obsessed with sin. It is all we talk about. We think that if we could just stop sinning we would be okay. As a result, we have developed a "stay-out-of-the-garbage" approach to the Christian life. Here we are, starving spiritually, God has offered us His "cafeteria line," and all we think about and hear taught is, "Stay out of the garbage. Don't eat the garbage!"

Are you ready for a really shocking statement? *The goal of the Christian life is not to stop sinning!* If it were, God would be asking us to produce the Christian life through obedience to the law. He asks us to live by faith because obedience to the law can never produce the Christian life.

According to Galatians 3:21, can the law impart life to you and me?

_____

Where is the power of sin, according to 1 Corinthians 15:56?

_____

If we are under the law, what are we under the power of?

_____

In Romans 7:7-9, how did Paul find out what sin was?

_____

What did he find out through the law that said, "Do not covet"?

_____

_____

What did sin produce in Paul's life?

_____

_____

What gave sin its opportunity to produce covetous desires in Paul?

_____

_____

What happened to Paul when sin sprang to life?

_____

In Romans 7:10, what did Paul think the commandment was intended to bring?

_____

_____

What did it actually bring?

_____

According to Romans 7:5, what aroused our sinful desires?

_____

What kind of fruit is produced by living under the law?

Based on these verses, can you produce the Christian life through obedience to the law?

What will be produced in your life by living under the law?

The "stay-out-of-the-garbage" approach to the Christian life doesn't work. The very thing we are trying to stop—sin—is the very thing we end up producing. The "power of sin is the law." The law not only doesn't stop us from sinning, it actually stirs up more sin. The problem is not with the law, though. It is with you and me.

That is why the goal of the Christian life is *not* to stop sinning. Even if we stopped sinning, there would still be something wrong with you and me. And that is the purpose of the law. It shows us who we are—spiritually dead sinners—so that we will turn to Christ for His life.

How Do You Look on the Inside?

In chapter 9 we learned that under law God's standard of righteousness is perfection. Jesus showed us in the gospels that this perfection is not only outward but also includes the heart. That is why the law cannot produce the Christian life. The law deals only with externals.

Read Matthew 23:25,27,28.

Who was Jesus talking to in these verses?

What did Jesus say the teachers of the law were like on the outside?

_____

What were they like on the inside?

_____

According to 1 Samuel 16:7, what does man look at?

_____

With what is God concerned?

_____

According to 2 Corinthians 3:14,15, when we try to produce the Christian life through the law, what covers our hearts?

_____

When is the veil taken away? See verse 16.

_____

Can the law change our hearts, based on the above verses?

_____

Who alone can change the hearts of men?

_____

Warnings to the Legalists

As we have already learned, the law stirs up sin in our lives and does nothing to change our hearts. This is what the law is supposed to do so that we will turn to Christ by faith. Either we learn the lesson the law is teaching us about ourselves, or we continue to hang on to the law and say to God, "I can do it!" To those who hang on, the law will either lead them into hypocrisy, or to outright rebellion. And like Marge, whose story we shared in chapter 9, they will eventually crash and burn.

In Galatians 2:12,13, why did Peter draw back and separate himself from the Gentiles?

_____

_____

Who was he trying to please: God or the circumcision group?

_____

What did Paul call Peter's actions?

_____

Look up the word "hypocrisy" and write out the definition.

_____

_____

What did Jesus call the Pharisees in Matthew 23:27,28?

_____

Why do you think the law makes people hypocrites?

_____

_____

According to Galatians 5:2-4, of what value is Christ to those who live under the law?

_____

If you choose to hang on to the law, how much of it are you obligated to keep?

_____

What two things happen to those who are trying to be justified by law?

_____

_____

Is there any hope of ever being justified by law?

_____

The Real Goal of the Christian Life

What was it that the starving man in our illustration needed? Real food that only the cafeteria could provide. What is it that every human being needs? The life of Christ! We need to experience daily the reality of knowing Christ and walking with Him in a vibrant relationship. The Lord defined eternal life this way: "Now this is eternal life: that they may know you, the only true God, and Jesus Christ, whom you have sent" (John 17:3). That is the real goal of the Christian life: *knowing Christ!*

Read Matthew 11:28-30.

When we are weary and burdened, where are we to go?

_____

What will Christ give us?

_____

How does Matthew describe the yoke of Christ?

_____

How does the yoke of Christ compare to the yoke of the law? Look up Acts 15:10 and Galatians 5:1 for the answer.

For what has Christ set us free?

How can we remain free to experience the life of Christ?

It takes only one law to spoil the entirety of God's grace. You can't trust in what you do and in what Christ has done at the same time. Our greatest need is to know Christ, to have Him dwell in our hearts. And His life can be experienced only by faith. It is only in comparison with the riches of knowing Christ that sin begins to lose its appeal; in fact, sin becomes stupid.

We are beloved, accepted children of God, who have been called to His "banquet table" to experience Jesus Christ living in and through us every day. Abundant life is real, and it is ours for the taking if we will only believe. Let's not settle for anything less.

11

. . . .

Living by a
Higher Law

. . . .

Motive Makes the Difference

At a seminar, David raised his hand to ask a question. "Bob, I can't quite get a handle on what you mean by 'legalism.' Certainly God wants us to do good things. And He doesn't want us to steal, or lie, or punch anybody out. What makes something legalistic or not legalistic?"

David asked a good question. You may be asking the same question. Why you do what you do is the first factor that determines if something is legalistic or not. Remember: Behind law and grace is the issue of God's acceptance. For example, one person's motive for witnessing is that he feels he must to gain God's acceptance. Another person's motive is because he is already accepted, and he is witnessing out of a genuine love and concern for people. The same activity occurs outwardly, yet the first man is living under law and the second is living under grace. The motive makes the difference.

The Key That Unlocks the Door

The love and grace of God is the true motivation for the Christian life. But my experience just didn't match up with the quality of life that is described in the New Testament. This issue was brought to a head while I was writing a series of Bible-study booklets on daily Christian living. I breezed through the first four lessons. The last lesson was to be "How to Love." Trying to write it was one of the most nerve-wracking experiences of my life.

Finally, God got through. "Bob, did it ever occur to you that the reason you're not able to write a lesson on love is because you don't know anything about love?" God was right. It seemed that God wanted me to go back to square one and start all over. I went back to lesson one, and there God taught me about His unconditional love and acceptance. Learning God's love for me was the key that unlocked the door.

Where does love come from, according to 1 John 4:7?

_____

What does 1 John 4:19 say is the reason we are able to love?

_____

If we do not know God's love for us, will we be able to love other people?

_____

According to 1 Corinthians 13:1-3, what are we without love?

_____

List the characteristics of love listed in 1 Corinthians 13:4-8.

_____

_____

_____

Is this type of love a feeling, or an attitude exemplified by certain actions?

_____

How are we to love one another, according to John 13:34?

_____

What does 1 John 4:8 say that God is?

_____

How does God love you and me? Substitute "God is" for "love is" in 1 Corinthians 13:4-8 to answer.

_____

_____

_____

What did Christ's death demonstrate, according to Romans 5:8?

_____

_____

When I went back to square one—Christ's finished work on the cross—I began to see His unconditional love and acceptance at a depth I never dreamed possible. Soon this love became real in me and I started experiencing Christ's love toward other people. As I responded to His love, His love became real in me.

A Lesson From Real Life

As God was showing me these truths about His love in the Word, He taught me what they meant through a real-life situation. One morning I gave my teenage daughter, Debbie, the chore of picking up the peaches in our backyard. She didn't do it, so I asked her why and she said, "There were bees out there." For some reason that answer sent me into a rage. "There are bees out there every day," I yelled. I ranted and raved, totally lost my temper, and made a complete fool of myself.

Feeling guilty and embarrassed, I went into my bedroom and got down on my knees to ask God for His forgiveness. This is what I had always done, but that day my prayer seemed empty. In my heart, it was as if God was saying, "Bob, I have already forgiven you. What do you think I did 2000 years ago?"

I took a different angle in my prayer. "But Lord, I am so sorry for losing my temper."

"Are you really sorry, Bob?"

"Oooh, Lord, I am really sorry!"

"Then go tell Debbie."

I nearly choked. "I'm not that sorry."

The struggle went on in my heart for the longest time, but I finally caught loud and clear what God had been teaching me for months. "Don't you see, Bob, that the problem is not between you and Me? The problem is between you and Debbie. If you love Me, then go be reconciled to her."

What does Matthew 5:23,24 say is more important to God: offering your gift at the altar, or being reconciled to your brother?

_____

_____

How did God reconcile us to Himself in Christ, according to 2 Corinthians 5:19?

_____

_____

If God reconciled us to Himself by not counting our sins against us, how then are we reconciled to each other?

_____

_____

How does John define God's love for us in 1 John 4:10-12?

_____

_____

What is our motivation to love one another?

_____

_____

How is God's love made complete in us?

_____

_____

Reread the story of Debbie and the peaches.

What was God more interested in: me asking Him for forgiveness, or me being reconciled to Debbie?

_____

In this situation, how would God's love be made complete in me?

_____

_____

What does Galatians 5:6 say is the only thing that counts?

After my internal struggle, I got off my knees and went back to Debbie's room. I looked at her and said, "Debbie, I'm sorry. I acted like a man who doesn't even know the Lord. Please forgive me."

That day I learned what it meant to have God's love made complete in me. Now all this was occurring just a few months after my desperate prayer offered while driving down the freeway to work. I had prayed, "Lord, take me back to the days when I first knew You." He was doing that and more. Finally, I was learning that God's priority was not my performance or knowledge, but it was "faith expressing itself through love."

Be Filled with the Spirit

"Be filled with the Spirit." Most Christians have heard this phrase and know that it is an important aspect of the Christian life. But it is here that many Christians become frustrated. I hear them exclaim, "I have heard this phrase all my life, but I don't have any idea what it means. Everybody says to do it, but nobody tells me *how* to do it!" I have experienced the same frustration. So what does it mean to "Be filled with the Spirit"?

With what does Paul contrast being filled with the Spirit in Ephesians 5:18?

When you are drunk with wine, what controls you?

Instead of being controlled by wine, by whom does Paul say we should be controlled?

_____

Read Ephesians 3:17-19.

What does Paul pray that we will have?

_____

_____

What do we need power to do, according to this passage?

_____

_____

What is the result of knowing the love of Christ that "surpasses knowledge"?

_____

If you are filled with the knowledge of God's love and grace, what controls you?

_____

_____

Can you be "filled to the measure of the fullness of God" and not be filled with the Spirit?

_____

_____

So what does "being filled with the Spirit" mean?

_____

_____

The Love of God and Deluxe Cheeseburgers

God's love working in our hearts deals with us on a level of sensitivity that neither law nor self-discipline can ever reach. An incident with my son, Bobby, taught me this personally.

Each Sunday our family went out for lunch. It started out as a fun, family time, but usually ended up with tension in the air. I began to wonder why. Bobby was 10 at the time, and he really liked going out to restaurants. What irked me, though, was that Bobby could never just order a regular cheeseburger. He had to order the "deluxe cheeseburger." And every week I bawled him out for ordering the most expensive item on the menu.

As I was praying, it seemed that God and I were carrying on a conversation in my mind about Bobby.

"Bob, how much would you like Bobby to spend on lunch?"

I had a figure in mind, so I said, "Lord, about $2.25."

"Bob, how much is a 'deluxe cheeseburger'?"

"Well, Lord, about $2.75."

"Bob, let's say that you go out to eat every Sunday. So subtract $2.25 from $2.75 and then multiply that figure by 50."

I did. I got a piece of paper and figured out the difference. It came to about $25 for the whole year. I felt so stupid. I had been hurting the feelings of my son over a measly $25. I got up and went home to tell Bobby that I was sorry, and that I would never hurt his feelings again for ordering a deluxe cheeseburger.

What was God trying to teach me through this incident?

_____

_____

How important is a decision about cheeseburgers in this world?

_____

How big is a decision about cheeseburgers to God when it is affecting a love relationship?

_____

_____

Could any law, except the law of love, have taught me that I was hurting my son's feelings?

_____

According to Galatians 5:13,14, what were we called to?

_____

How should we use our freedom?

_____

_____

How does Paul sum up the entire law?

_____

If the law is summed up in a single command to love others, how do we fulfill the law?

_____

_____

According to Matthew 5:17, what did Christ do with the law?

_____

How do you think He fulfilled the law?

_____

_____

From reading Romans 13:8-10, how do we fulfill the law?

_____

_____

How can we bear the fruit of love in our lives, according to John 15:5?

_____

If we are to love others, what must we know and rely upon, according to 1 John 4:16?

_____

It was only the love of God that could teach me to love my son and to quit hurting his feelings because he ordered the deluxe cheeseburger. Decisions about cheeseburgers aren't that important in the world's eyes, but God used this issue to teach me His priority that we love one another.

The Lord Jesus Christ said, "All men will know that you are my disciples if you love one another" (John 13:35). There's only one way that it will ever happen: We must first receive God's love and grace or we will have nothing to give. But if we receive God's love and become channels of that love to others, we can walk in the assurance that we are fulfilling the highest purpose of God in our daily lives.

12

· · · · · · · · · · · · · · ·

Freedom in Dependency

· · · · · · · · · · · · · · · ·

How Big Is Your Faith?

George was a conferee at one of our training seminars a few years back. He was blind and had numerous other physical ailments due to a diabetic condition. Although George's health was a constant burden, that wasn't the source of his greatest struggle. George wrestled daily with the belief that God had rejected him.

George told me his background and the teaching he had been under. His church taught, "If you have faith, you can do anything." The pastor made comments from the pulpit like this: "If you get cancer and die, it's your own fault! You just don't have enough faith!" Each week someone would place a hymnal in George's hands and say, "Maybe today, George, you'll have enough faith to see. Maybe today you'll have the faith for God to heal you."

George could never work up enough faith to be healed. After years of trying, he was a beaten, hopeless man.

Obviously, God must hate him, he thought, because he was a "man of little faith." George had believed a lie about faith and was in terrible bondage. The principle of "truth sets you free, error binds you" is no joke.

What George was taught about faith was not faith at all. The Bible tells us that "if you have faith as small as a mustard seed" you can move mountains. It can't be the size of our faith that matters. But what does it mean to walk by faith?

Let's begin by defining what faith is not.

Faith Is Not a Feeling

What does God tell us to do in the midst of anxious feelings, according to Philippians 4:6,7?

What does presenting your requests to God result in?

Is faith the action taken (presenting your requests to God), or the feeling that follows?

We have already learned in chapter 2 that emotions are responders to whatever we are thinking. Emotions come and go. That is why the Bible has very little to say about our feelings. Many people associate feelings with faith. As we saw in Philippians 4:6,7, exercising faith may result in feelings, but the feelings themselves are not faith.

Faith Is Not Intellectual Agreement with Doctrine

In James 2:17-19, how does James describe faith that is not accompanied by actions?

_____

How does James say he shows his faith?

_____

_____

What do the demons believe?

_____

Is what Satan believes about God enough to save him?

_____

Is intellectual belief in God enough to save us?

_____

According to James 2:21,22, how was Abraham considered righteous?

_____

What was the relationship between his faith and his actions?

_____

_____

How was his faith made complete?

_____

_____

Intellectual belief is not true faith. If I said to you that I believed a chair would hold me up if I sat in it, would I be exercising faith? Only when I sit in the chair is my faith made complete. Faith includes the elements of dependency and reliance, and always responds to truth with action.

Faith Is Not a Power to Manipulate God

How did James describe Elijah in James 5:17,18?

What was the result of Elijah's prayers?

Read Deuteronomy 11:13-17.

In this passage, what did God say He would do if Israel worshiped other gods?

Did Elijah decide on his own to pray that it would not rain, or was his prayer based on what God said would happen?

Who was the true initiator of Elijah's prayer?

I cannot manipulate God to do what I want Him to do. This is presumption. In true faith, God is always the initiator, and man is always the responder. God says something is true, and man responds by acting on it, depending on God for the results.

The Faith of Jesus Christ

We are told in the Bible that we should follow in the steps of Jesus. His life was an example for us to imitate. This seems impossible until we look at the humanity of Christ. Jesus always has been, is, and always will be God. But when He lived on earth, He lived as a man. And His life is our example of what living in dependency is all about.

In John 14:8-10, Philip asks Jesus a question. What is his question?

_____

_____

How did Jesus answer Philip?

_____

_____

Where did Jesus say the Father was?

_____

_____

Were the words that Jesus spoke His own?

_____

How did Jesus explain His life?

_____

_____

Whose work was being accomplished through Jesus?

_____

How much could Jesus do by Himself, according to John 5:30?

_____

> For I did not speak of my own accord, but the Father who sent me commanded me what to say and how to say it. I know that his command leads to eternal life. So whatever I say is just what the Father has told me to say (John 12:49,50).

From what is recorded in John 12:49,50, did Jesus speak on His own accord?

_____

Who told Jesus what to say?

_____

To what do the Father's commands lead?

_____

So, what does Jesus say?

_____

_____

_____

As recorded in John 14:16-20, who did Jesus say He would send to live in us?

_____

What is the reason we live?

_____

What will we realize about our relationship with Christ when the Spirit comes to live in us?

_____

_____

How does our relationship with Christ compare to Christ's relationship with His Father?

_____

_____

Jesus Christ lived in total dependency on His Father. Every day Jesus presented His humanity to His Father as a vehicle to express the life of God to the world. All that Jesus did was the result of the Father doing it through Him. Therefore, He could say, "Anyone who has seen me has seen the Father" (John 14:9).

Freedom in Dependency

A "life of total dependency" is an elusive concept for people to grasp. The best explanation I have heard has been expressed by Major Ian Thomas in what he calls the "threefold interlock." A life of faith is our *love for God* resulting in *dependency upon God* resulting in *obedience to God*. This pattern is clearly seen in the life of Jesus Christ.

The first commandment of the law was "Love the Lord your God with all your heart and with all your soul and with all your mind" (Matthew 22:37). Only Christ fulfilled this commandment. As a result of that love for His Father, He lived the life of total dependency that we have already seen: "By Myself I can do nothing." This resulted in a life of perfect obedience, crowned in the Garden of Gethsemane where He prayed, "Father, if you are willing, take this cup from me; yet not my will, but yours be done" (Luke 22:42).

As beloved children, we are called to live according to the same pattern as the Lord Jesus. It is only as we approach the Christian life in the correct order that we will experience the true freedom and life that God has purposed for us.

What enables us to love God, according to 1 John 4:19?

_____

What must we concentrate on in order to love God?

_____

_____

Can you depend upon someone who loves you?

_____

In John 15:5, who does the vine represent?

_____

What are we?

_____

Does a branch produce fruit or bear fruit?

_____

What produces the fruit on the branch?

_____

_____

_____

When we abide in Christ, what results in our lives?

_____

How much can we do apart from Christ?

_____

According to Galatians 5:22,23, what fruit is produced in our lives when we are abiding in the vine?

_____

_____

Apart from having a heart that is truly learning to love God, we will have no motivation for obedience other than abject fear of punishment. On the other hand, apart from an understanding of what it means to live dependently, we will have no ability to live obediently. A lack of understanding in either of these areas leads inevitably to a return to the law. Apart from God's pattern, we have no motivation or power for true obedience.

The love of God is our motivation. The life of God is our power. Our responsibility is to maintain a dependent, receiving attitude—the same attitude that Jesus presented to His Father for 33 years—and Christ will produce the fruit of His life in us.

Raise Your White Flag

Christians of all camps agree that obedience to God is the desired goal. How you become obedient is the problem. God has made it clear that legalistic obedience without a surrendered heart is worthless to Him. He is looking for an attitude that says, "Lord, I can't, but You can." He is looking for an attitude of total surrender.

It's like those old World War I movies. In the midst of furious trench warfare, bombs exploding, and machine guns crackling, a small white flag is raised in surrender. "Do with us whatever you please. We give up," they are saying. But when we surrender, we surrender ourselves not to the enemy, but to a loving God and Father, who will take charge of our lives in His perfect wisdom and control.

Read Romans 12:1,2.

What is our spiritual worship?

_____

_____

What is the motivation for offering ourselves to God?

_____

_____

After we offer our bodies to God as a living sacrifice, what does Paul tell us to do?

_____

_____

How are we to be transformed?

_____

What will renewing our minds enable us to discover about God's will?

_____

_____

What is God's will for you and me, according to 1 Thessalonians 5:18?

_____

_____

Are we to give thanks in both good and bad circumstances?

_____

What can we thank God for, according to Romans 8:28?

_____

What attitude does Philippians 4:6,7 say we should have when we present our requests to God?

_____

What guards our hearts and minds when we are depending on Christ to work our circumstances for good?

_____

What does an attitude of thanksgiving express about your dependency on God?

_____

_____

When you have a thankful attitude, who are you recognizing is in control of the situation: you or God?

_____

A life of dependency is characterized by the attitudes of surrender and thanksgiving. As we adopt these attitudes, we begin to see life from God's perspective and not our own. And there we experience the peace of God that passes all understanding.

George made the decision to give thanks and trust the Lord to cause even his blindness to work for good. Through placing his total dependency upon Jesus Christ, George found Him to be all He claimed to be—the answer to every need of the human heart.

13

Growing in Grace

You Can't Go Back

It's been more than a decade since the day I was driving down the expressway with tears streaming down my cheeks and crying out to God to restore the joy of my salvation.

My prayer at the time was, "Lord, take me back to the days when I first knew You." God's answer did not lie in going back; the answer was to go forward. With what He has taught me about His love, grace, and what it means to be alive in Christ, today I wouldn't want to go back.

I was much like the Israelites after Moses had led them through the Red Sea. God told them to enter the Promised Land where they could eat from trees they did not plant and drink from wells they did not dig. But because of unbelief, they would not enter into what God had promised. Afraid to go ahead and unable to return to

Egypt, the desert was all they had left with its boredom, monotony, and dryness.

I couldn't go back to the days when I first knew Him. Those days were gone. I could either enter the Sabbath rest God called me to—resting totally in the truth of God's unconditional love and grace—or live in the desert. Like the Israelites, I settled for second best.

We try to make the desert flashy and exciting, like a "spiritual Las Vegas." It looks pretty on the surface, but it's nine miles wide and one inch deep. It's sometimes exciting, but deep down you know the desert is not the "abundant life" Jesus promised. For a while I was content with all the glitz and flashy show-biz approach to the Christian life, but after a time it became old.

I am thankful today that God allowed me to go through that desert experience. He answered my cry—not by taking me back, but by bringing me to a newness of life that I never could have imagined.

The Promised Land

Like the Israelites, God has prepared for you and me a promised land called a Sabbath rest. Our rest is not found in a land, but is found in our relationship with the living Christ. God has always had a remnant of people who have said, "Lord, I'm not satisfied with the same old thing. I don't want to practice a religion; I want to know You in a real relationship." To the hungry ones, to the humble ones, God will always respond by leading them into true freedom.

In Matthew 7:7,8, what does Jesus say to do to those who are hungry to know Him?

_____

_____

What is the assurance we have when we ask, seek, and knock?

_____

_____

Read Genesis 1:27–2:2.

What did God create on the sixth day?

_____

After He created man, what did God say about His creation?

_____

After God created man, was His creation complete?

_____

_____

Is there anything that man could add to God's work of creation?

_____

What did God do on the seventh day?

_____

Why were the Israelites unable to enter the rest of God, according to Hebrews 3:18,19?

_____

How do these two verses define "disobedience"?

_____

_____

According to Hebrews 4:9-11, what remains, then, for the people of God?

_____

What do we do with our works when we enter the rest of God?

_____

In creation, God did all the work. There was nothing that man could add. So it is in salvation. God has done all the work through His Son, Jesus Christ. There is nothing you or I can add. God wants us to grasp by faith the fact that Jesus Christ has done it all, and realize that there is nothing left for us to perform to be acceptable to God. In other words, "God has done the work; now you rest."

This "resting" is not the same thing as being inactive. I can't think of anyone more active than Jesus Christ. Just as Christ rested in the fact that it was the Father doing His work through Jesus (John 14:10), so too, we can rest in the truth that it is Christ living His life, doing His work through us. When we make ourselves available to God, we will be more active than ever, but the work is Christ's.

In Philippians 2:12,13, what does Paul exhort us to continue to do?

_____

_____

_____

Does Paul say to work *for* our salvation, or work *out* our salvation?

_____

For what reason are we to work out our salvation?

_____

_____

Why does God work in us?

_____

_____

So whose work are we working out?

_____

What is the mystery of the Christian life, according to Colossians 1:27?

_____

_____

Whose workmanship does Ephesians 2:10 tell us we are?

_____

_____

What were we created in Christ Jesus to do?

_____

_____

What if the president of the United States called you one day to ask if he could use your car. Without hesitation you would say, "Yes!" You would wash and wax your car, and change all your plans just to make your car totally available to the president.

As Christians, the God who created this universe lives in us and wants to use our bodies every day of our lives to show His love and grace to the world around us. Think about it: God lives in you and wants to produce fruit through you that will endure for eternity! I can't think of a better reason to approach life with contagious enthusiasm.

It's Not That Complicated!

In spite of the fact that it is full of good news, classic Christianity is resisted and met with objections, usually in the form of "buts" and "what abouts?" "I know we are under grace, but..." and "I know we're totally forgiven, but..." and "I know Christ lives in us, but..." I call it "billy-goat Christianity": but, but, but. We are simply afraid to believe that God really means what He says.

We have complicated the Christian life with all of our "buts" and "what abouts?" But Christianity is not nearly as complicated as we make it.

According to Galatians 2:20, who do I have living in me?

_____

How are we to live this life in the body?

_____

In whom is our faith, and why?

_____

_____

Based on 2 Corinthians 5:14,15 (NASB), what controls us?

_____

Since Christ died for you and me, for whom should we live our lives?

_____

If you are angry at another person, what does Ephesians 4:31,32 say to do?

_____

_____

How are we to forgive others?

_____

Do you know how someone is going to respond if you go to that person to try to be reconciled and settle the issue?

_____

Because of God's love for you, can you trust Him with the results?

_____

If you are tempted to steal to provide for your needs, what does Ephesians 4:28 say to do?

_____

What can we trust the Lord to do when we seek first His kingdom, according to Matthew 6:33?

_____

How does God promise to meet our needs, according to Philippians 4:19?

_____

The Christian life is not nearly as complicated as we make it. God calls us to simply live by faith. When faced with a specific situation, motivated by the love of Christ, it becomes a simple matter of presenting your body to Christ and trusting Him to live His life through you. And in the specific situation you merely do by faith what the Bible says and leave the results to Him.

Growing in Grace

We are strongly urged in the Word of God to go forward aggressively and lay hold of all that God has prepared for us. We are called to grow in grace. Christ has come to live in us and has promised to complete the work He began (Philippians 1:6).

If Christ lives in you, you can't live in sin without tremendous internal conflict. If you are a butterfly, you will never be happy with the worms again! And since God is committed to conforming His children into the image of His Son, He can be counted on to apply appropriate, loving discipline to get them back on track.

Based on Proverbs 3:11,12, what should our attitude be toward God's discipline?

_____

Whom does the Lord discipline?

_____

What is the attitude of the father toward the son?

_____

Read Hebrews 12:7-11.

What is God treating us as when He disciplines us?

_____

If you are not disciplined, what does that tell you about your sonship?

_____

For what purpose does God discipline us?

_____

_____

In what does God's discipline allow us to share?

_____

When we have been trained by it, what does God's discipline produce in our lives?

_____

_____

What should our attitude be in the midst of trials, according to James 1:2-4?

_____

_____

What does the testing of our faith develop?

_____

How does perseverance finish its work in you and me?

_____

_____

Discipline is an issue we must settle for two reasons. First, because Jesus said, "In this world you will have trouble" (John 16:33). Second, because when faced with the trials and tribulations of life, there is no human tendency stronger than to ask the questions, "Why did this happen? Is this problem a sign that God is angry with me?"

A Great Cloud of Witnesses

The Book of Hebrews was written to Jewish Christians who were facing tremendous pressures and trials. They were being barred from the temple and synagogues, they were being ostracized and threatened, and many were wavering in their faith. The writer of Hebrews writes to encourage them: "No, God has not rejected you. Don't give up. Keep on going." To help them, he points to example after example of those who have walked by faith throughout biblical history.

Read Hebrews 11:33-35.

List all the things these saints of old accomplished through faith.

_____

_____

_____

_____

_____

Did the circumstances of these saints change for the better because of their faith?

_____

Read Hebrews 11:35-38.

List what happened to these saints who walked by faith.

_____

_____

_____

_____

Did their circumstances improve or get worse?

_____

For what were all these saints commended, according to Hebrews 11:39?

_____

_____

What was important to God: their circumstances—whether good or bad—or their faith?

_____

In light of this, how should we look at our circumstances, whether good or bad?

_____

_____

Into what have we gained access by faith, according to Romans 5:2-5?

_____

Standing in grace, in what do we rejoice?

_____

In what else should we rejoice?

_____

_____

What does suffering produce?

_____

_____

What is the end result?

_____

Why does hope not disappoint us?

_____

_____

Our trials and tribulations are not a sign that God has rejected us. We stand in His grace, and there, whether our circumstances are good or bad, we are loved and accepted unconditionally. When trials come, accept them as an opportunity for God to build into you perseverance, character, and hope. The end result is that God will pour out His love into your hearts by His Holy Spirit.

So don't give up. As Peter said, "Grow in the grace and knowledge of our Lord and Savior Jesus Christ" (2 Peter 3:18). You will not be disappointed.

Conclusion

• • • • • • • • • • • • • • • • •

Whatever Happened to the Real Thing?

• • • • • • • • • • • • • • • • •

Developing a Godly Perspective

Sharon called me on "People to People" one night. "I'm learning more and more about God's love for me," she said. "But I have a situation I don't know what to do with." She paused and took a deep breath.

"I am 19 years old now, but when I was younger, I was sexually molested by four of my uncles. Since then I've come to know Jesus, and I don't hate them anymore. I've forgiven them. The problem is when I see them at family reunions. I feel so uncomfortable, and I don't know what to do."

We discussed the promise in Romans 8:28 that "God works for the good of those who love him, who have been called according to his purpose." Then I asked her a question. "Sharon, do you think you will run into any other women in your life who have been through a similar experience?"

"I'm sure I will," she answered softly, her voice breaking as she tried not to cry.

"This is a sinful, sad world, and bad things are going to happen to people," I said. "Sharon, the best possible person in the world to minister to those women with the love and compassion of Jesus is *somebody who has been there*. In this world, we are going to have trials and tribulations. We cannot escape them. But God uses these to teach us compassion so that we can reach out to others. That's how God works our circumstances together for our good."

Sharon got the message and began to see herself and her circumstances from God's perspective, rather than from her own.

How does Paul describe God in 2 Corinthians 1:3-5?

_____

_____

Why does God comfort us in all our troubles?

_____

_____

With whose comfort do we comfort others?

_____

Based on these verses, how does God work things together for our good?

_____

_____

Knowing that God comforts us in our troubles, and gives us compassion to reach out to others with the love of

God, can you see the reason why God tells us to "give thanks in all circumstances" (1 Thessalonians 5:18)?

_____

Christ, Who Is Your Life

How could Sharon simply let go of the very understandable emotions of bitterness, hatred, and self-pity? There is only one way: by developing a totally new mindset, a new preoccupation. We are not able to let go of things until we have something new to hang onto.

Read Colossians 3:1-3.

Since we have been raised with Christ, on what should we set our hearts?

_____

_____

Where is our life now hidden?

_____

With what should we clothe ourselves, according to Romans 13:14?

_____

Who is to be our primary concentration?

_____

In Ephesians 4:22-24, what are we taught to do regarding our former manner of life?

_____

_____

How are we made new?

_____

_____

What are we to put on?

_____

_____

What is this new self created to be like?

_____

What does Matthew 20:28 say that Jesus came to do?

_____

_____

If we are preoccupied with Christ, what attitude will He be developing in our hearts?

_____

_____

What attitude does Philippians 2:3 say we should have?

_____

According to Galatians 5:13, what characterizes the true life of freedom under grace?

_____

_____

The unmistakable sign that "Classic Christianity" is taking hold in a man's heart is when you see the beginnings of the same attitude that Christ had: "I am not here to be served, but to serve." There is nothing less natural to a human being than that attitude. Only the miracle of the gospel can produce it. As we set our hearts and minds on Christ, He will teach us the joy of serving others. And like Sharon, we can have the experience of reaching out to others with the same love we have received from Christ.

Whatever Happened to the Real Thing?

The title of this chapter is a question: "Whatever Happened to the Real Thing?" The answer is, "Nothing!" There is nothing at all wrong with the message! Neither is there anything new about the message of God's grace. When it is shared straight and undiluted, it transforms lives in the same dramatic way that it did in the early days after Pentecost. The problem is not with the message—it is with us. We have strayed from the simplicity of devotion to Christ into religion and legalism.

But God keeps calling us back to Himself. Like Sharon and George, when we come to Him we find Him to be the answer to every need of our hearts. God opens the floodgates of His love to any man, woman, boy, or girl who comes to Him in humble faith. The Lord continues to say to you and me:

Here I am! I stand at the door and knock. If anyone hears my voice and opens the door, I will come in and eat with him, and he with me (Revelation 3:20).

Listen, open the door of your heart, and discover that Classic Christianity is a Person—the living Lord Jesus Christ.

A Personal Invitation

• • • • • • • • • • • • • • • • •

If after working through the *Classic Christianity Study Guide* you realize that you have never accepted God's offer of salvation in Jesus Christ—or if you simply are *not sure* whether or not you are in Christ—I invite you to receive Him right now. John 1:12 says, "to all who received Him, to those who believed in His name, He gave the right to become children of God." In Christ is total forgiveness of sins, total acceptance, and eternal life.

Salvation is a free gift that you accept by faith. You are not saved by prayer, but prayer can be a way of concretely expressing your faith in Christ. For example, here is a suggested prayer:

> *Lord Jesus, I need You. Thank You for dying for the forgiveness of my sins and for offering me Your righteousness and resurrected life. I now accept by faith Your gift of salvation. Through Your Holy Spirit, teach me about Your love and grace, and about the new life that You have given me. Begin the work of making me into the person You want me to be. Amen.*

Again, there is nothing magical about praying these words. God is looking at the heart that trusts fully in Him.

If you have received Jesus Christ after working through the *Classic Christianity Study Guide*, if your life has been impacted in other ways through the ministry of this book, or you would like more information about our ministry, I would very much appreciate hearing from you. Please write to me, Bob George, c/o People to People, at P.O. Box 1009, Argyle, Texas 76226. May God bless you with a deep personal understanding and experience of His matchless love and grace!

For every vibrant, fulfilled Christian, there seem to be nine who are "doing all the right things" but still feel bogged down, tied up, or burned out. What is missing?

Classic Christianity
by Bob George

Why do so many Christians start out as enthusiastic believers and end up merely "going through the motions"? Drawing on his own struggles and years of teaching and counseling experience, Bob cuts right to the heart of why Christians sometimes end up disappointed and unfulfilled in their Christian walks.

Have you ever struggled with the questions:

- **What does it mean to have Christ living in me?**
- **How can I experience the joy of the Lord daily?**
- **If I'm a new creation, why do I still struggle with sin?**

In his down-to-earth style, Bob George shows us the answers to these questions *and* the way back to authentic Christianity—the kind that Christ had in mind when He set us free.

Every sincere seeker can get back on track and experience true abundant living. Life's too short to miss the real thing!